An Imprint
Not Forgotten

THE INTROSPECTIVE POETRY OF
BRIAN K. FRASER
VOLUME II

AN IMPRINT NOT FORGOTTEN:
THE INTROSPECTIVE POETRY OF BRIAN K. FRASER, VOLUME II
Copyright 2021 Brian K. Fraser
All rights reserved.
Edited, designed, and published by EMPATH BOOKS, LLC 2021
New Mexico, USA

No parts of this publication may be reproduced, stored in a retrieval system, or transmitted in any form or by any means, electronic, mechanical, photocopying, recording, or otherwise, without the prior written permission of the copyright owner.

This book is sold subject to the condition that it shall not, by way of trade or otherwise, be lent, resold, hired out, or otherwise circulated without the publisher's prior consent in any form of binding or cover other than that in which it is published and without a similar condition including this condition being imposed on the subsequent purchaser. Under no circumstances may any part of this book be photocopied for resale.

Cover art by Bridget Hochman. All rights reserved.

ISBN# **978-1-7367282-1-5**

AN IMPRINT NOT FORGOTTEN

TABLE OF CONTENTS

1. The Old Man's Observations
2. The Wave
3. Time for Kathy
4. Living with Your Love
5. Your Dearest Friend
6. Sharing My Colors
7. A Choice of Sincerity
8. Uncertainties I Await
9. You've Come Thus Far
10. All That Is New
11. Not By Chance
12. Reviewing My Mind
13. My Routine
14. No Fees Were Charged
15. My Playground Mind
16. Love Allows No Greed
17. Beauty Seeks Experience
18. I Said Hello
19. Charlotte's Web
20. The Rose You Missed Yesterday
21. Cherished by Few
22. Nothing on My Mind
23. If Love is Not Found
24. Nurse Debbie's Dilemna
25. The Warmth That You Pour
26. Living in the Struggle
27. Masks
28. Memories That Will Not Last

29. I Missed Another Part of You
30. I'll Follow Your Path
31. The Dream I Never Had
32. Before I Knew the Sun
33. Sanity That Scatters
34. Challenging the Strange
35. The Love That Makes You Blue
36. An Imprint Not Forgotten
37. Searching to be Free
38. The Seemingly Unknown
39. Steps of Summer
40. The Love You Do Not Stake
41. All In Love Is Fair
42. Some of What I Heard Is Nothing That You Said
43. My Discovery
44. Missed You
45. A Breathing Cure
46. Stitches of the Loom
47. I Want You to Know
48. The Life That Once Was
49. In Losing What I Found
50. In That I'm Lost
51. Listen
52. The Reward
53. Know What I Send

An Imprint
Not Forgotten

I

The Old Man's Observations

The old man bitches and complains about things gone down.
He puts a weight on my load, with his familiar sound.
He tells me how it was, how it used to be,
How "Big Brother" corrupts, how he used to be free.

When he was young and in the Second World War,
He said the country pulled together to settle the score.
The troops came home and the nation was free.
He was then, on his own, away from the insanity.

But does it ever leave you, the brutalities of war?
Do you ever wake up at night fighting for the door?
Although the men are home and the war is won,
The burden of your victory is a very private one.

The rest is really sketchy--I'm not even sure--
But he married the woman he loved, the love he had was pure.
They lived many happy years together, before the final sigh.
The war had started up again, the day his wife had died.

Is it the inner turmoil? Have the dreams returned?
His wife is gone, his job is done--nothing left to learn.
He talks about the "good old days," with a gauge that makes me wince,
And complains of aches, pains and operations that've happened ever since.

Maybe he's trying to prepare my future by the difficulties of his past,
But this young man already understands the futility of his task.
I listen to his problems, his weakness and his pains,
And learn from his mistakes, his losses and his gains.

His script is already written, he wants nothing new to know.
He feels his life is jaded, while telling me to grow.
I wish he'd open up his mind and try to understand,
Instead of grunt and moan at me, for trying to be a man.

For this excursion, what more do I need?
In my life I've seen assassinations of the free,
Lost loved ones, and experienced a disease of the mind.
I listen to the old man cry, while trying to be kind.

Maybe he sees me as unlearned, while I'm trying to be optimistic.
Maybe I see him as crass, while he's trying to be realistic.
The confusion of this predicament lies between the generations.
The gap is not in time, but in the old man's observations.

                                                      6-19-1992

2

The Wave

No questions, no wonders, and nothing to do,
But reign with comfort in this place that you view.
No heartbeat that flutters, no breath that you save.
No cries to utter until after the wave.

The scream was the doubt, the voice not your own,
And you, the life that this love had sown.
Helpless and yearning for the love that they gave,
Yet the tides were turning, before you knew the wave.

Now, I have no idea. Only you could tell
If you weathered the storm before the swell.
But the love you found in the water so brave
Made you consider its wonder…to ride the wave.

You must have been eager—curiosity's zest.
Your dedication to excellence finds you seeking the best.
Your desire to challenge this life that you pave
Helps you balance your questions when you teeter the wave.

Does it matter to know the water's not kind--
That the sea shows its will when the oceans unwind?
Yet still you will be there, facing its stave
With another encounter to merge with the wave.

These words could go on forever, until the waters still,
Or you could trace the moon to find the perfect thrill,
And ride on nature's shoulder, still knowing that you crave
Another chance at life, before you know the wave.

You have a chance to share what the water's given you---
The breath of love's beginning is *loving what you do.*
You've given a life of comfort--so is your art engraved.
Your true test in life is transcending the wave.

I, too, face this challenge, but do not know your quest.
The water is the flow, the land is its arrest.
The life is in the loving—love beyond the grave—
Love that's everlasting—caressing the wave.

11-4-1992

3

Time for Kathy

Pleasing others pleases you.
You're always thinking of the right thing to do.
Do you spend your time thinking about what's right or wrong,
Like you do when you're learning the notes to a newly found song?

What motivates your desires when you find something all your own?
Is your first thought to share this treasure you've sown?
Maybe it was a gift for you, and you only.
Would not giving it away leave you alone and lonely?

I remember you told me of a hurt from your past.
You asked me to keep it to myself, and I have.
But my concern for you, Kathy, is why I write today.
I've waited too long to hold back what I'll say:

You've the best of intentions and your ways are all right.
You'll smile at the worst of them to avoid a fight.
But the fight that you're having is waged from inside,
For when you look within, there's nowhere to hide.

I see you observing the beauty this world can present,
And watching you grow, I find nothing to resent.
But, Kathy, please trust me, for the years that I've had:
You're not alone in your fears. Please don't be sad.

If you share with me your worries, I won't go away.
If you say, "Mind your own business," for you I'll still pray.
'Cause I know you're a wonder, and I love your way,
And my future's a blessing for knowing you today.

So now you have a treasure to keep, all your own.
It's words from my heart, and love that I've known.
It's all those who love me, who love you, too.
What's been so freely given to me, I give to you.

11-22-1992

4

Living With Your Love

I say, "I love you," just because,
But it's more than that, that I'm thinking of--
For you told me what you saw, before I told you.
You recognized the feelings I thought nobody knew.

It seemed you didn't have to study, you didn't have to share.
Revealing what you did, I knew you had to care.
And only in my shoes could the price be so great,
Wondering in my steadfastness, "Would it be worth the wait?"

But it wasn't in impatience for this reality, that I sought,
For only in the waiting did you see the virtues that you caught.
It verified my existence--that it wasn't done in vain.
To really experience the pleasure, I must encompass the pain.

Was it only just a test, or a manifestation of a need?
Does Mother Earth understand her search for a seed?
And when the blossom of this search yields a flower unknown,
Will the bee that makes its visit, ever really know its home?

I thank you for your time and the love that you expressed.
It wasn't just coincidence--this sanctity I caressed.
Admitting in fear the events and shame of your past,
I embrace your trembling candor. It's today that has the grasp.

I hope you will remember me, not as in times before,
But in the presence of your moment, to even the score.
For time and space are only obstacles to all of the above.
In living without you, I'm living with your love.

1-8-1993

Your Dearest Friend

Open the door and look around
At all the beauty that you have found.
Gaze through the windows of your abode
And cherish the moment, before it erodes.
This life inside that you helped create
Finds no fault in you, or your mistakes.

Say hello to your friend, and leave no doubt:
This is who knows what you're about.
And when you cry to someone, but nobody's there,
Your friend is busy mending those wounds that you bear.
When you find yourself healing from this pain you don't
    understand,
Your relief is just beginning to lend your friend a hand.

Your friend is your love, that knows you so well,
That sees you through life—your heaven and hell—
Only asking you to love yourself again,
To leave behind the memories your mind has made a sin.
I have a friend who loves you, no matter what you're stuffing,
'Cause he knows that you're beautiful, capable and loving.

5-1-1993

Sharing My Colors

Worlds together, worlds apart,
Conflict begins when confusion starts.
I know you're trying, you're doing your part.
I'm sorry my crying offended your heart.

Did you ever wallow in the fear of losing a friend,
And misplace all your values from beginning to end,
Only to realize, amidst your virtues and your sins,
That loving one who does not care is loving amends?

If I gave you a rainbow, you'd be happy 'til the sun went down,
But the moon would then light the stars all around,
And the sky would rejoice, with your gaze it had found.
In your bliss, you'd jump for joy, while the rainbow hit the ground.

The colors to your rainbow have all merged into one.
The darkness of the night caused the colors to run.
There's a pot of gold at the end of the rainbow to come,
But you can only find it when the night yields the sun.

I will not take a color from the rainbow that you hold,
But I will add a hue, if I could be so bold.
You may not see it in your spectrum, these values that I mold,
Yet I feel better for sharing my colors, before I get too old.

6-25-1993

A Choice of Sincerity

Whatever your expectations in this life, so far,
You'll never fall short of who you are.
Whenever the love you sought is not there,
You may look within, without despair.
I can see your beauty, without the light.
I can see your love, without my sight.

And I partake in your love, though you may not know,
'Cause I give it back to you, though it may not show.
For you share the wonder in your own life's mistakes,
And expose the blunders that your errors create.
I find here no fault, because I'm human, too.
In praying for me, I'm praying for you.

So you may ask me what prompted this poem,
But don't wander far, for your thoughts may roam.
It's not an obscurity, with a dilemna unclear.
It's a choice of sincerity, in telling you, dear:
My friend you are. With love, I share.
Because you are. Because I care.

7-7-1993

8

Uncertainties I Await

Once again you come around,
Struck again, with a familiar round.
You're here to heal, by my way you're bound.
You'll stay long enough to regain your ground.

So I redirect my love, concentrating on your fears,
I listen to your woes, while you resurrect your tears.
I give to you my time, still questioning my years,
And think of you in a different light, by calling you, "My Dear."

Can you sense what I am saying while you come around again?
I'm not a martyr for your question marks, a debtor for your sins.
I'm a searcher of a seeker, who wants to be a lover and a friend.
I'm a train without a track, where the tunnel's not the end.

Can you feel what I'm saying without the talk it sometimes takes?
Can I be your friend and not your lover, by claiming no stakes?
Can I love you regardless of the rules I do not break?
Or is my love a proposition to the uncertainties I await?

Maybe I'm a stepping stone toward the places you are going,
A temporary hiatus on the river that's still flowing--
Nourishment to the child, whose love still frets from growing,
On the way back to the beginning of the seeds that she's been sowing.

I am not bitter, where others might be riled.
I can't contain your freedom. Mother Nature reconciles.
My freedom is my love. Some think it's running wild.
Please be careful with my heart, for I am, too, a child.

8-8-1993

9

You've Come Thus Far

So to this point, you've come thus far,
And maybe still, you wonder about what you are.
Are the desires you hold still intact,
Or is the fear of this day striking you back?

When you labor in the day with the friends you know,
Do you think it matters to them that we age when we grow?
For if time is our enemy, then how can we change?
What you learned today, yesterday was strange.

Forget about your years, while you greet this day.
Don't fret with your fears, for your fears will stray.
Rather, be grateful for this time that you have.
We celebrate your birth as happy, not sad.

A mother you are, and a wife to a man.
Your husband and your children have no better plan.
And strive you will, in school, to learn even more.
The success of your attempts adds credence to your lore.

I was asked to share my words with a friend I sometimes see.
Facing a new decade, one with less complexity.
Sharon, it's your birthday, so lighten up and be.
May happiness be kin to your newfound reality.

9-9-1993

10

All That Is New

I have come to seek all that is new,
But nothing grows old, when I'm thinking of you.
You're a constant memory in the present tense,
An accumulation of time that has no since.

I see your face, yet I cannot stare.
I hold you and love you, but you're not there.
I'm confounded with confusion, 'cause I'm not really sure
If what I am, you are, or what you are, we were.

So I honor these tidings, but I do not grieve,
And I surrender to love, for it will not leave.
Having taken a chance, and been gifted with you,
I have come to seek all that is new.

9-24-1993

II

Not By Chance

How wonderful it must be to see your world spin,
From the tips of your toes to the freedom within.
All those years of dedication to dance,
And someday you'll premiere…but not by chance.

Grace is not found, it's acquired by work.
The rhythm inside is never a quirk.
How do you feel when your world's a stage,
When the moves you make are the critic's gauge?

I also see your moves in the place you're employed.
It's a dance that I thoroughly enjoy.
There's no mistake in doing what you do,
Dancing is your love, and love is what you do.

9-27-1993

Reviewing My Mind

It's 3 a.m., when the Sun doesn't shine,
And I can't sleep while reviewing my mind.
I upset your day by committing a crime:
I made a commitment, but stole your time.

It's not that your time means nothing to me.
God gave it to you, God gave it to me.
Our lines crossed, and that's reality,
But did you use your time constructively?

I see you as one who cares about others,
Like the sisters of mine who love their brother,
Like strangers who smile and greet one another,
And those who write of follies, so they don't have to smother.

Please accept these apologies that your rationale greets,
And allow me forgiveness the next time we meet,
For I am learning from the lessons that teach.
And thank you, Jean, for cleaning my teeth.

10-8-1993

My Routine

I'm working on a routine where I don't have to think,
Where the charade of problems is the missing link
To the confusion and misery lying on the brink
Of disaster so feared—but I will not sink.

Only when I *ponder*, do I think something's wrong.
It's a break in my music that interrupts my song--
An unanticipated distraction, a moment too long,
When introspection demands, *"What's going on?"*

And when I look inside, I must break through a cloud,
For all I didn't ask for lives within this shroud.
Inside all this conflict, in visions, so loud,
Is where I court the junction, and battle the crowd.

Beyond this circus is where I have found
The mirror inside, in circular round--
Perceptions without deceptions, reality astounds--
Connections with directions selflessly abound.

I cannot stay long, for the music returns.
I remember the songs and the lessons I've learned.
But my routine is different and I can't discern
If I think too much, or my routine is too stern.

10-12-1993

14

No Fees Were Charged

No prices were paid,
No fees were charged,
And I have stayed
While you were "at large."

It's not a guilt I pass to you,
For I am always "passing through,"
Taking notes on what can be,
So I can share the best of me.

It's alright when it's all wrong,
'Cause I'll just sing another song.
But without memories for words I sing,
It means not much of anything.

Please recognize that I do not know
How hard it is for you to show
The part of you, beneath control--
The heart of you, above your soul.

And you may think I ask too much
For I, too, fear the human touch.
I hope it's not a burden to tell you I care.
If you were only hungry, with food, I would share.

But the nourishment you're lacking can never be replaced,
And the memories you cherish will never be erased.
I find some consolation in living as we do--
In quiet desperation, we find another view.

So I tell you "I love you," and your fears arise again.
Acceptance is a challenge, when reluctance strives to win.
No stakes were set, still the cards were played,
Hand by hand, trade by trade.

We looked at the cards and risked the scars,
Cause no prices were paid, and no fees were charged.

10-19-1993

15

My Playground Mind

Give until it hurts, till the hurt goes away.
Love until you cry, cry until you stay.
I give away this love I dare not try to hold.
In loving only me, the future's getting old.

If you cry for your love and your tears hit their mark,
The love that returns may be pity from their heart.
And pity without love lacks the growth that mends--
A prerequisite for love is not to expect what you send.

So how do I know what your touch can do for me,
If I love only the you that I see?
And why isn't it enough--this vision of your being?
Because my mind *forgets* what my sight is healing.

The distance between us is closer, in my head.
The more I imagine, the more I have said.
'Cause we get along in my playground mind--
I never cry, and you are always kind.

Love is never the end, at the beginning of this quest,
For it has always been, it's never had a rest.
And if the time should come that I tell you how I feel,
You will know my truth, and I will know what's real.

11-16-1993

16

Love Allows No Greed

You cannot walk, before you crawl.
You can't pick yourself up, before you fall.
You can't play the game, if you stall.
You can't see the truth, if your window's a wall.

Blinded by the beauty that others possess,
I find myself reaching for the very best,
Not knowing that what they have is apart from the rest--
That they have what they want, is anybody's guess.

Show me what I want, so I can find what I need,
For my heart may not follow the path that you lead.
And if I say, *"I love you,"* this is my creed:
"Love, for the sake of love, allows no greed."

This will all be forgotten, for time marches on,
But I took the time to notice—a moment too long.
My questions yield answers that all seem wrong,
With solutions so complex, I hear my own song.

You will grow, but you may not see
What it means when it is said, *"love is free,"*
Not, *"If I do for you, will you do for me?"*
But to say *"I love you"*—mean it, and let it be.

11-28-1993

17

Beauty Seeks Experience

Whispers in the dark, a cloak you cannot find,
Softly spoken words, hidden in the rhyme.
Sounds beneath the surface, seeking their own time,
Mellow as they murmur messages that chime.

Beyond the obvious, you may never know
What to keep, and what to throw,
What's forgotten--because it shows--
And that which is obscure--until it grows.

First you see it, but then it's not there.
Do your eyes deceive you, or do they care?
Or did you see what can't be seen, even if you stare?
Beauty seeks experience, for those of us who dare.

All the thoughts you never heard, and thoughts you almost had
Lie in an oasis of nakedness that's clad.
In sight, we seek distinction and judge it good or bad,
But in beauty lies extinction, a happiness that's sad.

2-11-1994

18

I Said Hello

When I first saw you, you were aloof,
For friends you had--I saw the proof.
And friends you'll be, with friends you have.
You shared your thoughts, you shared your laughs.

Then I saw you sitting all alone,
Hiding tears you thought only you had known,
Writing down words in a letter to him,
Wrestling with the destitution growing within.

I know that place. It's a solo pain.
You swear you'll never trust love again,
But love is pure, and pure is free.
No chains contain your destiny.

I greeted you. You were still feeling low.
I said, "I love you," but you heard "hello."
You said it was done, over and through.
You told me you saw him, now, in another view.

Someone's thinking about you, as the curtain falls.
If nobody takes a risk, everybody stalls.
I said, "hello," but you were feeing low.
You said, "I love you," but I heard "hello."

2-14-1994

Charlotte's Web

I'm tired and weary, and not sure how I feel.
I'm hopelessly in love with everyone whom I deal.
I'm not really sure if you understand what I say,
But your response to me has indicated your way.

And you might wish that I could change,
'Cause you might like to rearrange,
For you are the flower and I am the bee.
I fear that you think what I take is for free.

So give me your pollen and I'll protect my Queen.
Keep your fantasies and I'll keep secret my dreams.
You carry the fruit I use to make honey.
I love you for you, and not for your money.

I need not remind you; you keep me in my place.
You tell other flowers where I stand, in this race.
And when they hear the words that you say,
The close up their petals and hide in the day.

2-28-1994

20

The Rose You Missed Yesterday

Committed and faithful to a flock not your own,
But your desires are elsewhere--maybe your home.
I see you in silent regard, to thoughts far away,
Yet I do not probe your wonder or get in the way.

Was it something you forgot, or something left undone?
Is there a picture in your mind of the beauty yet to come?
Do you feel removed from the presence that surrounds you--
Contemplating arenas of mysteries that confound you?

But that's not all I see, as I watch you in motion.
To tell you the truth, you cause me commotion.
I'm never prepared for the emotions I feel,
And I always return to see if they're real.

So you see the best of my One Act Play.
The drama conceals the words I don't say,
'Cause I wonder about you--inquiries so sincere,
And while I court your wonderment, my mystery is fear.

There's falsity in believing, commitment in a lie,
Safety in perceiving that I shouldn't even try.
How can you answer the questions I do not pose?
In observing my selections, my confidence just goes.

I'm grateful to know you, though I never really said.
A love has thrived and fallen—all in my head.
And you may be somewhere gazing, wondering as you do,
But the rose you missed yesterday is today's love, coming through.

3-25-1994

21

Cherished by Few

A working woman, also a mother,
A single-child family, wanting another.
Does her daughter need a sibling--a sister or a brother?
Or does the father want a son to share with his lover?

With the times unsure and realities unseen,
Would another child complete the dream?
For the child you have is a beauty queen,
And the one you want captivates your means.

I envy what you have, but you carry all the weight.
No burden is your love, when time creates your fate.
You want unborn life, and you will have to wait.
The beauties of your life are yours by Fate.

I wish for you the best in all that you do.
The future is a task, one which is never through.
And the payback is your love, so cherished by few,
But I am one who sees it. I'm grateful for your views.

4-4-1994

Nothing on My Mind

Nothing's ever lost, and it doesn't go away.
It just gets left behind, like the seasons we betray.
Truth is only flattery, if faith has gone astray.
Faith must have an anchor to sensibilities at bay.
Fidelity is misery, if love we cannot find.
But yesterday's a memory of *nothing on my mind*.

How it was, is not how it was to be.
You were always there when the future was a dream.
When I looked ahead, I only saw the past.
Imagination's only fair until reality takes its grasp.
Now it's bits and pieces--the movie's but a scene.
I find my heart is reaching the limits unforeseen.

Compassion is decision, reaching for its crest.
So who are you, today? Whom do I caress?
These questions I live, but where is my home,
Caring for a love I cannot find alone?
It's for you I am wishing, you I do not phone,
You I can't be missing, for you, I've never known.

4-21-1994

23

If Love Is Not Found

It's the silence in time when I question the moment,
As if an observational pause warrants a comment.
The world is always moving, but when my mind stands still,
Love is all revealing, but fear is all I feel.

I take a chance with my life, when I share it with you.
The question is not love, but *will it be true?*
And it's always you who deems our direction.
When I take no risks, I risk no rejection.

It's really just a game with the rules undefined:
Desire with a meaning, regardless of the find.
But we will not be happy until we get to play,
Then we make the rules, to make each other stay.

I cannot be the answer to all you desire,
And you are not a stepping stone for my love, to hire.
If nothing's ventured, then nothing's gained,
But if love is not found, then life is feigned.

5-9-1994

Nurse Debbie's Dilemna

Part of my own is your own.
If this were not true, you would not condone.
You're at work while I'm away from home,
But you induce discipline, when your defenses roam.

I received a taste of your control tonight.
Do you possess altruism, or do you emerge from fright?
It's not one person that sets me this way.
It's his followers that agree with his dismay.

First there were four on a bench—true to all.
Then I entered and the numbers did fall.
Five were especially present, five in all,
But my friends left me behind, while the leaders stalled.

So I appeal to you, 'cause I respect your position,
And I realize you, too, are a follower seeking direction.
I only wish you would hear me out,
Because these words I write are what confusion is all about.

7-30-1994

P.S. Loneliness--a feeling of lack of love--got me here. Now I must again return to smoking and conversing with myself, alone. That is why you see me at the Nurse's Station a lot... I'm tired of being alone. Can you understand alienation?

25

The Warmth That You Pour

Many days I've held your love--
Held it in my hand, inside of a cup.
It's not the brew I'm speaking of,
It's the warmth you pour, that I'm drinking up.

Some days I awake to the rank and file.
From my imagination, this order is stealing.
Lately I arise anticipating your smile,
Let me tell you how your love is feeling:

I've never denied my yearnings to learn.
My heart is always open to the freshness of life.
But love isn't freedom if it has to be earned.
Questions emerge within your strife.

You are not on trial, let me tell you so.
Nothing's wrong with you, you're perfect as you are.
Fear not to share. This pain you bear, I know.
In reaching out, it's all about nourishing your scars.

Please don't flee the part of me that won't let you go under.
Let me share the lessons that life has given me.
I know it's not your plan, I know it makes you wonder,
But your love is not tainted. Your honesty can be free.

Now just allow time to do its work, as only time could.
Do not hold forever this pain that you are storing.
Let me hold the brew, and share with you what's good.
Give yourself a break. It's time I do the pouring.

8-26-1994

Living in the Struggle

Their world is without a goal to be,
They hunt for smokes and cash for coffee,
They share a world that only they know,
Drag their feet on the pavement: "Which way to go?"

Their dress is simple: whatever fits.
They cry for no reason, to regain their wits.
But what do we see, when we face our own fears?
Yet we cry that they're "freaks," say that they're "weird."

I have a friend who lives in this struggle.
She lives in two worlds, outside the bubble.
In one, she shares her fragmented plans,
Then looks at me to see if I understand.

Two children has she, under someone else's care,
She speaks of them, lights a smoke, and then stares,
I wish I could tell her my time was all hers,
But I know not time's way. I'm not really sure.

If she looks at you, while explaining a story,
Please listen to her--her moment of glory.
Look into her eyes, for her truth is within.
Then look in the mirror, and let it begin.

10-9-1994

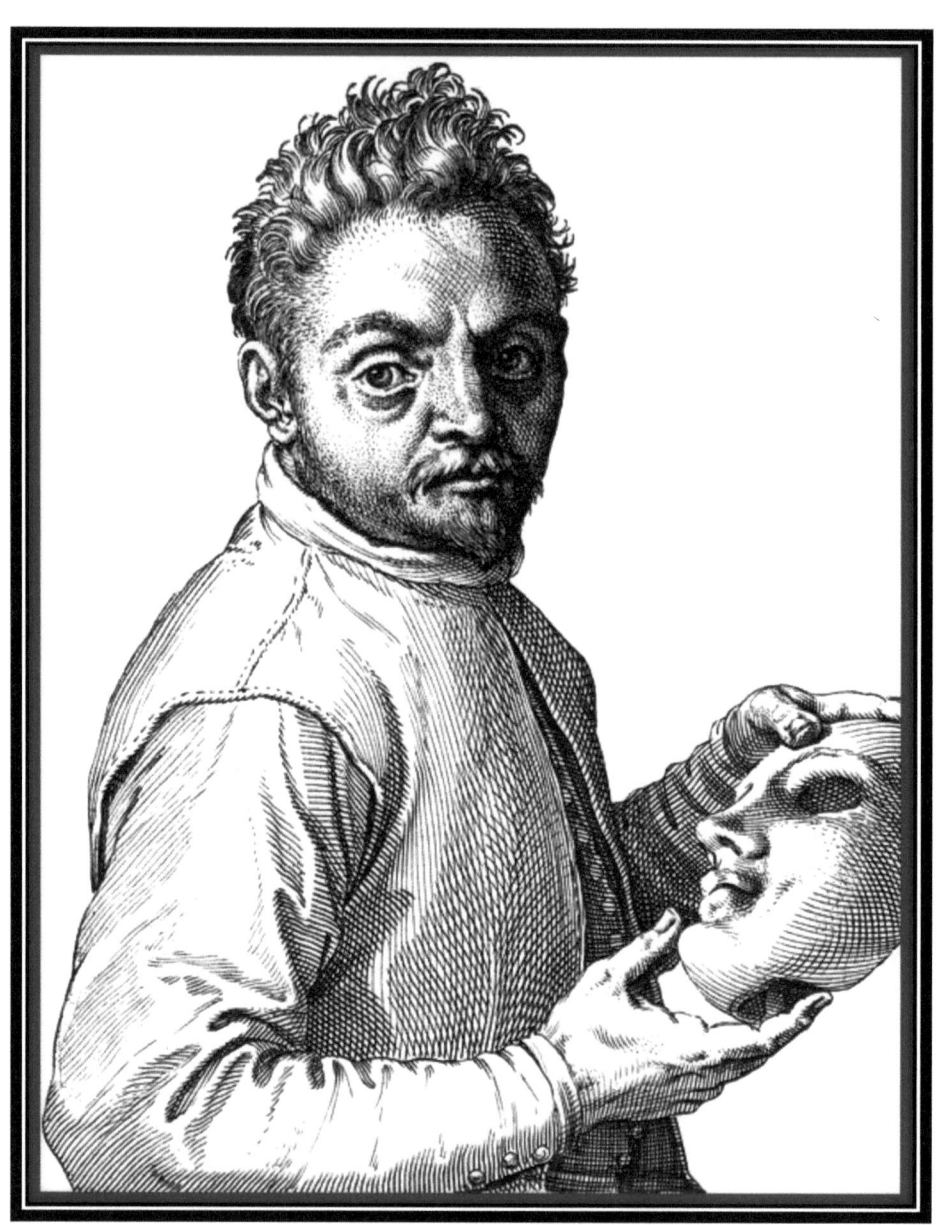

Masks

I wish you the best in all your endeavors.
I wish you time, long past forever.
I really wish that you could see
The mask I hold in front of me.
You think I'm honest; you tell me so,
But the mask gets heavier as I grow.

I say, "I love you," but what's this mean?
It means my mask is in a dream.
And I foresaw this happening time,
For I found love, when love was blind.
When the mask was tired and the words were free,
You caught a part of my reality.

You say, "thank you," or "I love you, too,"
But is this game really ever through?
I fear your shame when I consider this task,
For I must also go beyond *your* mask.
So many facades that we endure,
In search of a love that's not impure.

But love, my friend, is already here,
And we lack tact when our mask is fear.
Too much hurt from loves gone by--
I see your mask is beginning to cry.
The miracle of life is on the hunt,
'Cause when I share your tears, I lose my front.

11-11-1994

Memories That Will Not Last

Soon, these days and times will pass
And turn to memories that will not last.
We'll be different, but not know why--
Roll away a tear, instead of cry.

It's the times that are happening, I remember best--
Things we hold onto, amongst the rest.
And all we love, of all we knew--
We let it go, when we are through.

Let me cry for the time that will be gone,
For I know, now, that we live our song.
We are the lyrics, the music we sing.
Happiness clings to the love that it brings.

1-13-1995

I Missed Another Part of You

Did you ever wonder what could be
When the reflection of your eyes came back at me?
Did you ever wonder what would show
If I told you, "I love you," but did not know?

Open your eyes, but do not blink
And call our rhythm that makes us think,
So when we flinch beneath God, above,
It will be in unison and we'll miss nothing of our love.

And when you close your eyes to sleep,
It'll be me who takes another peep,
'Cause I'll take the visions of what we are
And give it to my own private star.

One heart plus one heart equals one heart.
When yours slows down, I'll pick up your part.
But when I flinch, will your heart hear
That I missed another part of you, my beloved one, my dear?

1-21-1995

I'll Follow Your Path

Seemingly beyond the scope of the world within
Lie answers to questions that will not end.
You smile reassuredly, and say, "Let it be."
You speak your truth. I seek my reality.

I guess it's the longing that keeps me here,
For what I lack, of what I fear.
Your world is content, your questions are few.
With more to be done, there's even less to do.

I'll follow your path when the answers are none.
I'll have no questions when dark is the sun.
I'll love you forever and not even ask why,
For I feel your hurt, and I hurt when you cry.

There still seems to be another suggestion:
When I feel for you, I forget my questions.
The questions are gone when the reality is you.
In finding you here, I know what to do.

2-27-1995

31

The Dream I Never Had

The dream I never had was the dream I never missed.
The fury of the fantasy was realized in a kiss.
I gaze upon my hands clenched into a fist.
Letting go is always slow, considering this bliss.

You were never gone, and I was always there.
Keeping in mind that, *in love, all is fair.*
To know you is to feel you. To see you is to bear
Longings for togetherness--coupled, if you dare.

Tomorrow is a long time, 'til you remember, it's today.
Memories of yesterday have wisdom to convey.
And time is just a marker, when love has its own way,
Crying to get darker, to greet another day.

The kisses were enough, as I wake up to the new--
The newness of my life--the newness in my view,
Bewildered in my wondering, but knowing that it's true:
The dream I never had was the time I spent with you.

3-29-1995

Before I Knew the Sun

For my sister, Jeanette

You are my oldest sister, the one I most cheer.
You're in my heart; when we're apart, I hold you near.
You sing my songs and still my fears.
You continued to love me through my confusing years.

But a life of your own do I see,
Yet not without all—including me.
Do I deserve your loving for free?
Your love is the shade of my Family Tree.

You took on a love you were sure was fair.
It wasn't that way, but still you cared.
Your love brought you a daughter to bear.
Growing inside you, it softened our despair.

She was innocent beauty with love's domain,
And you were her mentor—a sisterly reign.
She loved life so much, that I can't explain.
Let's thank God for her time, for I must refrain.

You were a single mother with a solo plan
To raise your daughter alone, but you didn't understand
That God was working overtime, and I was a fan.
Your daughter saw a father; you loved and married the man.

You loved your "Babe," but you had to know
His growing pains would have to show.
You held onto him through a blinding snow,
You questioned yourself, so you both could grow.

And your daughter got a sister to share the chores,
So you and your husband love life even more.
It's a lifelong job. I've yet to open that door,
But you give me hope for my dreams in store.

This poem is never-ending, the thoughts forever undone.
The sentiments of my past have presently begun.

The sibling that I've looked to, since before I knew the Sun,
Gave to me a light, from which I did not run.

5-23-1995

Sanity That Scatters

Time goes by and my observation changes.
In seeking new surprises, my vision rearranges.
No longer do I ask you about things I think you know.
Rather, now, I want to feel the things that do not show.

It's easy to accept you when I see what makes you happy.
It seems easy to accommodate, trying to please your quandary.
But I lose myself, where your contentment is my goal,
And I forget about my heart, mind, body, and soul.

Giving it all away like nothing else matters,
Trying to hold it all together with sanity that scatters--
Every moment, I'm a newborn, trying to be heard,
But you don't see me struggling, as you hold on to these words.

I'm not a pessimistic cynic, nor an optimistic fool.
Beyond this kaleidoscope of disarray, love's reign still rules.
In the beginning, I was seeking you, and found myself instead,
'Cause I realized my fantasies were realities in my head.

7-20-1995

34

Challenging the Strange

I wonder how the delicate negotiate the change,
Leaving the life they had, challenging the strange,
Fearing if they go back, it will all remain the same?
But nothing's similar to dying, and dying is the shame.

You are a budding flower that foresees life again.
You trusted in the weather and almost met your end.
You emerged beneath a darkened cloud, searching for a friend.
I give to you my love. With love, to you, I send.

You say you wonder how it will work, with the changes you have done.
The answer's in your faith. Your faith must not succumb.
And when you start to meet your self, do not turn and run.
The image that you cherish is the one that's just begun.

I'm a little older, but no wiser than you, dear.
We harbor similar outcomes, but we dwell in different fears.
I'm trusting in the process. I drive so God can steer,
Confronting my fragilities, I ask you to be near.

I wonder how the delicate negotiate the change,
Leaving the life they led, challenging the strange,
Fearing if they go back, it will all remain the same,
But nothing's similar to dying, and dying is the shame.

8-23-1995

The Love That Makes You Blue

You'd better figure your wants along with your needs.
You can't grow your garden while holding your seeds.
You give what it takes, but you take it all back.
You want what you need, *but you need what you lack*.

I have what I have, I give what it takes.
I love what I have, make no mistakes.
I love you--and that's my concern.
Do you love what you have, or love what you've earned?

Someone's going to stumble and someone's going to fall.
Fearing what we do, we answer to the call.
I cannot separate my boundaries, when the circle is within,
As you do not know where you will go when the uncertainties begin.

So hold onto your seeds, for my garden will still grow,
And hold onto your needs. It's your wants that need to know:
Is the love that you are sharing the love that will be true?
Or is the love that you are missing the love that makes you blue?

9-27-1995

An Imprint Not Forgotten

When the tides seize and the sun doesn't shine,
When the wind stops, when the words don't rhyme,
When the clocks freeze and there is no time,
I'll say, "I Love You," where there is no crime.

But there is no Sun, so there is no light,
And no wind will carry my words in flight.
With no time to pass--no day or night,
I only feel, *"I love you. You're out of sight."*

For the beauty of this moment
Is that it will never be, again.
This is not a mere illusion
With no beginning, or middle or end.

Between the daily things I do,
My mind returns to you often,
In the déjà vu of a memory--
An imprint not forgotten.

So I review this confusion that's devoid of space,
And retrace my connections in search of a place
Where there are no trespasses, nor sin—only grace--
Then the illusion becomes a reality: your smiling face.

10-25-1996

Searching To Be Free

I have to look at memories to avoid reality's pain.
You were a friend in comfort--of this I cannot feign.
In prayer we were together. Hope and faith were gained.
Answers to my questions were your questions, once again.

More of these, less of those--this one's got to stop.
I hope you're feeling better now, battling those thoughts.
Our sanities are feelings, played on different lots.
The lid to this confusion is on another box.

This is how it feels when the mind won't let you be.
This is what I know, of my friend and me.
I have lost a comrade who was searching to be free,
But kept her prayers and hopes, the freedoms that agree.

I'm sorry for her family, though time will have its way.
The hurt and pain of sorrow will show us what to say.
And love will come together for those sanities that stray,
And I will remember Carol, who touched me when we prayed.

11-10-1996

The Seemingly Unknown

I venture out once more, to the seemingly unknown,
To a place where I have hurt--a place where I have grown--
And I fear the future's outcome, for the present still feels safe,
But reality's a trick of risks I do not take.

You tell me you want more, but I know what that entails.
If I match my love with your desires, it'll be my honesty that fails.
When my sincerity in giving carries what it steals,
I'll see the pain of loving is not what love reveals.

And I know that I find comfort in the love that I possess,
But I feel it should be harnessed toward a soul I can caress.
If I give my love only to your wants and your desires,
I'm missing what I'm loving, and loving what expires.

1-29-1997

Steps of Summer

We joined your world to find you in happy resolve.
Your journey has been marked, though you are still involved.
We were with you on your walk, but for your walk to be true,
You must walk the steps of summer, still waiting for you.

For you must surely know that summer leads to fall,
And fades away the season, like your dreams in withdrawal.
The books upon your shelf may remind you of age,
But history can be cunning, while in the turning of the page.

Time in its season is the rhyme of the reason.
Your dedication to now is love without treason.
And your ride on the trail is your horse's trek, too.
Success without love is like one without two.

I celebrate your success, but I know that you're not done.
I believe in your completions, though they've only just begun.
And I'll walk with you this summer, but you can't see me there,
'Cause my steps were laid years ago, learning how to care.

Happy Graduation, Cassandra

6-20-1997

40

The Love You Do Not Stake

I say hello to you, but you consider the world first.
The now is in the moment, but you contemplate its worth.
Reality is fleeting, while you take a hold of a scene.
I'll say hello again, but I'm speaking to a dream.

You have so many choices, yet only one way to go.
A part of you rejoices, and a part, you do not know.
There's safety in your being and lack that will arise.
I can relate to what you're missing, while gazing in your eyes.

Tend now, to the meaning, for the words can lose their way.
All that you are searching for is that which you dismay.
Take a chance at gaining the desires you detour.
Never in your reluctance will ever you be sure.

You thought you had "it" once, then wondered if it was.
You broke away the ties, and went away because
You found you didn't love him--a love you could not take.
The "it" that you are yearning for is the love you do not stake.

I know you have commitments, I know you feel a loss.
The path of your resistance is shadowed by its cost.
While you know what is right, you sense what is wrong.
Love may not seem near, yet love is never gone.

I must now retire from the words that I have used,
For I do not aspire to make your scene confused.
When I say "hello," I mean it's the easiest word I can find--
Clothed within its essence is *"I love you,"* not far behind.

6-27-1997

All In Love Is Fair

You left me today, but I'm not sure what I miss--
Is it the love that I cherish, or the love that I resist?
For all that I have given is all that I have had.
It's insane to think I'm losing a love you think is sad.

It's all give and take, till we say goodbye.
It hurts to leave. It helps to cry.
And I will always wonder, but I'll never really know
If the love I think I miss is the love that will not go.

So do what you will, for I don't fairly know my part.
My love is not a bargain--an investment in your heart.
The freedom of this game is not a contract of your will.
How could I think you're leaving me, determines how I feel.

I wonder if what I'm attracted to is really all my own,
And searching for, in you, a place to make my home,
A selfish way, indeed, to court loneliness' despair?
But only is it lovely, when all in love is fair.

10-30-1997

42

Some of What I Heard is Nothing That You Said

*For a friend I met in counseling,
who inspired me to heal, but eventually died from his addiction*

Dear Jim,

If you only knew what you meant to me,
My dream would be so different from what I see.
Some of what I heard is nothing that you said.
We shared an inner pain that lingered in our heads.

Though my youth was curtailed by the confusion of my will,
I always returned to my passion, and you were there, still.
I said, "I quit," but you said, "No such thing."
So I pursued your truth* and finished my dream.**

I arrived long enough to again encounter my pain,
Then you shared with me your hurt, confusion, and shame.
Younger was I than you were, in that "place,"
Then I was a colleague to what my mentor would face.

Did it help for you to know that I had suffered, too?
Did we identify a bond, understood by few?
You had so many who loved you by choice,
Still, I knew the familiarities heard in your voice.

Now that you have left us, the lesson remains clear:
All that I have fought, is for all that I hold dear.
And when I think to where I almost said my suicide goodbyes,
My reflection could not bypass my feeling of knowing you had tried.

9-22-1998

*He believed in the importance of having a dream, and wanted to become a chef.
**I dreamed of achieving a stable sense of mental health.

My Discovery

To do it all alone would be a permanent blunder,
So I cherish our moments together with an alluring wonder.
You give more than I've ever known,
So I can share with you what I've never shown.
It's the story of your life that you share with me,
And I listen and learn as you reveal "my discovery."

You tell me your truth, honesty, and will.
I'm amazed at your candor, as I keep it in and feel.
And you don't have to give up your love for me to know
That I don't have to keep my love, for you to grow.
I thank you for your lessons, for the time you spent,
And we may feel that "misery loves company,"
But love is what we meant.

3-06-1999

44

Missed You

Dear Mom,

    Came by to say, "Hello."

    You're not home, I must go--

    Back and forth, to and fro.

    It's a Ferris wheel, this I know.

    Time and time again, it's so.

    I'll be back for another show.

    I love you, Mom and Dad.

Brian

4-7-1999

45

A Breathing Cure

There is no order when there are no plans.
There is no progress, till you take a stand.
Behind the shadow of indecision, lies a breathing cure.
It's not an answer that you seek, but to have it, as it were.

'Cause when you look ahead, it's your present that you see,
And the future seems to be today's reality.
Today gives you less of what you love and more of what you lack.
In deprivation's a reminder that just might send you back.

No one that you see is enough for what you had,
'Cause no one else can be the happy for the sad.
Memories can do no wrong, when love is what you feel,
And reminiscing can hide the memories you conceal.

So may you find the truth in loving what you miss,
For in your question lies the answer to your bliss.
It's not that it's unknown, it's just that it's untried.
The Life that you miss is the Love that has cried.

4-13-1999

46

Stitches of the Loom

Are you amazed at the questions you have not asked?
Do the feelings you have, ignore your grasp?
Are the answers unknown--the end of the line?
Is the future the end of the beginning of time?

Everything I know is all I ever had.
All that I regret is all to me that's sad.
And yours is a story I hope I'll never live,
But it's the story in your eyes I hope that you will give.

You're more to your mother because of his act.*
The courage you show is part of this pact.
I sense this belonging you think you'll never find
Has been with you, without him, for a very long time.

So try to protest this predicament's ruin,
And know you are creation--the stitches of the loom.
In trying to climb the mountains on the path already paved,
We tend to miss the flowers that love's already laid.

7-15-1999

Her father abandoned the family.

47

I Want You to Know

I want you to know,
I want you to see,
I want you to grow,
But it's not up to me.

My head is not lost,
My heart is not lame,
My dread is the cost,
My fears are to blame.

You are fine. You are perfection.
I see you strive, and I know why.
Yet the view I lack is your direction,
And the sights I see are all awry.

A *common bond* is what my heart does see.
 I could not share how it feels, alone.
The duty of two is the lack of the free.
Life is not empty, when love is at home.

So I see where life takes me, with an unconscious wish,
And I know where I go needs no question.
The food on my plate is the gift of the dish,
The uncertainty of knowing is the burden of affection.

The time has arrived and the truth, it is dear.
The answers are the questions that were never posed.
All that I know is out in the clear.
 I want you to know. I want you to grow.

11-17-1999

The Life That Once Was

The life that once was, the memories that are--
The Light that now is, was once a star.
All that you love, of all that you knew
Is all that there is, cherished anew.

If life were but a day and night was "The End,"
Would sunshine be love? Would darkness be sin?
As long as you see what you think you understand,
You place faith in the star, but not in the plan.

It makes no sense to me that we have shared a similar sight.
We were thrown together, to where our darkness yielded light.
And we can see what we dare not want to know,
But we are not the light, and darkness has no glow.

All that we love may have never been seen,
Had One not loved us, in spite of our schemes.
I know that you've loved, yet I know it's not lost.
The love that you share caused the darkness to pause.

1-13-2000

In Losing What I Found

The scenery has changed again, one more time.
Has my outlook strayed, or is my third eye blind?
Is my quest for loving lost in my head?
Or am I lost in seeking, feeling underfed?

When I find a comfort zone, the world has rearranged,
And I'm in contempt with Time--reality again strange.
The world was indeed turning, the moment I jumped on.
Did I miss a revolution, or is the resolution gone?

When I began my picture, modern was the art,
And subtle were the colors, until the psychedelic part.
The ride it put me on nearly took me out,
Yet the manner that it taught me is what I'm all about.

So if I reminisce, it's not because I miss
The dance of yesteryear, the momentum of the wish.
I may have lost the count, but I never missed a turn.
In losing what I found, I'm teaching what I've learned.

4-9-2000

50

In That I'm Lost

Which came first: darkness or space?
Where are we now? What is this place?
Are we weak, or are we strong?
Do we seek a common bond?

Do I "need you" because I don't know what I want?
Or do I "need you" 'cause I have nothing to flaunt?
Are you for me to see--for my sight?
Or are my visions enhanced by the light?

Do I feel, because I must?
Do I like, because I trust?
Am I here in search of you?
Or are we here only to pass through?

Indeed, what I've found is what I've got.
All that I know is all that I've sought.
It's because I am, that I know you are--
Enhanced by the light, begotten by the star.

So does it matter who we are, or why we live?
Or that we want, because we give?
Do we hurt in spite of pain?
Or do we lose because we gain?

This only matters because I have asked.
All that I know is all that I've grasped,
And all that I see is all that I feel.
Nothing is something, if everything is real.

I know I lack, and I know I stall.
I know I love, and I have it all.
But I do not know what love will be,
In that I'm lost, in that I'm free.

6-4-2000

Listen

Every time I find the way, I forget where I am.
Everywhere I look, I seek to understand.
All that you offer is all I'll ever need,
Until I change my mind, considering my greed.

The journey is the trip, the destination is the fuel.
The answer is the grip, the question is the duel.
I'm holding onto answers while the questions arise.
The sun is my light, until the moon arrives.

But nothing has it all, until something is seen.
The end is forgotten in creating the dream.
So I ask myself: *Should I stay where I start?*
I'll ponder this condition 'til I listen to my heart.

8-15-2000

The Reward

I'm going to learn what is up with the sky.
I'm going to search with the wind, as it sighs.
I'm going to receive your love, by and by.
I'm going to see where the lesson lies.

I have a dream, all tucked away.
It's in my heart, but in my way.
It won't reveal itself, to my dismay,
But leans toward fruition on another day.

You say, "Seek it out and follow your dream.
Find your truth and make it your scene."
As you count your fingers and lust, while you deem,
I wonder about the cost of this scheme.

Maybe living longer will open my heart.
The beginning of knowing is the end of the start.
And knowing my love is knowing my part.
The design for this life is the reward of its art.

9-19-2000

Know What I Send

Turn around to change your view
And try to catch what you threw.
Is what you cherish not your own?
Or is your love that which you have thrown?

All you know of all you've been told
Is all that's young and all that's old,
And in that moment, you are time.
Is what you give yours, or mine?

I seek not what I give, though it comes in return.
Did I give what I got, or did I get what I earned?
Is what I toss to the wind *gravity's burden?*
Or did I seize my love? Is it my love that's hurtin'?

I really don't know if it's you, or it's me--
If you are really happy, or if I am really free.
But the circle remains and the game never ends,
'Cause I don't' know what I love, but I know what I send.

11-26-2000

Brian Fraser

Also by this author:

 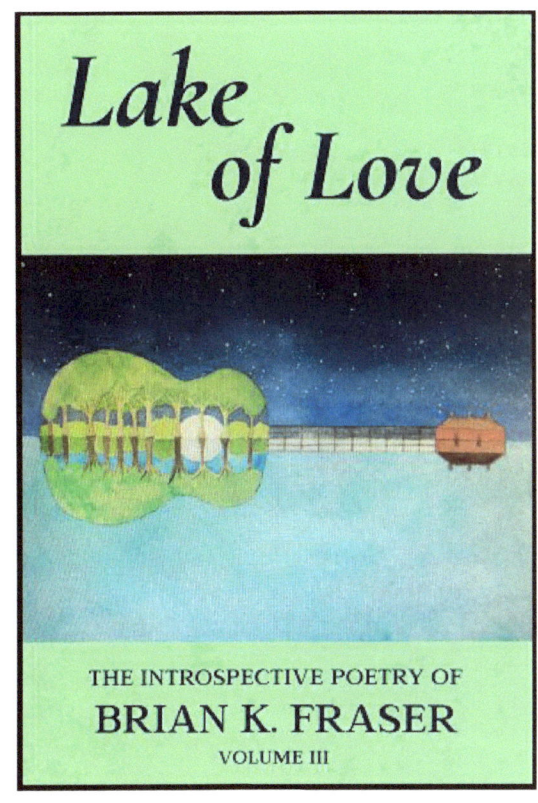

www.ingramcontent.com/pod-product-compliance
Lightning Source LLC
Chambersburg PA
CBHW041701160426
43191CB00003B/49